I SMELL SOMETHING FOUL

I SMELL SOMETHING FOUL

HAIKU EXPRESSIONS OF

EVERYDAY ANGST

by Alison Herschberg

Andrews and McMeel
A Universal Press Syndicate Company
Kansas City

I Smell Something Foul is produced by
becker&mayer!, Ltd.

ISBN: 0-8362-2141-9
Library of Congress Catalog Card Number: 96-86127

ATTENTION: SCHOOLS AND BUSINESSES
Andrews and McMeel books are available at
quantity discounts with bulk purchase for
educational, business, or sales promotional use.
For information, please write to:
Special Sales Department, Andrews and McMeel,
4520 Main Street, Kansas City, Missouri 64111

Text type was set in Fournier
Display type was set in Roughhouse
Cover illustration by Peter Georgeson
Book design by Trina Stahl
Book production by Devorah Wolf

To my endless sources of angst and inspiration:
Jackie, Stanley, and Sasha,
and the rest of my extended family
(you know who you are).

Introduction

HAIKU IS THE JAPANESE WAY OF saying, "Dig it, man," in seventeen syllables and three lines of verse. The haiku poem began in the sixteenth century as a form of comic social commentary, taking on the emerging middle class as its target for biting satire. A century later, the master Bashõ developed the 5–7–5 format for his more serious, classical poetry. Due to a glaring lack of automobiles and fax machines, Bashõ was inspired largely by his natural surroundings. These simple poems were observations of life, the Zen expressions of simplicity found in nature.

Today, nature is shrinking; city living requires inhaling the residues of toxic synthetic materials; and selflessness is becoming as obsolete as the royals. The classical form of haiku is enjoying a modern revival based on its original raison d'être—the decline of social and ethical values in favor of shameless self-promotion and unabashed righteousness. A slight deviation from its origins, perhaps, but a revival nevertheless.

Why is the haiku poem experiencing this sudden surge of popularity? Angst.

Without angst there would be no blues. Without angst the consequences wouldn't matter. Without angst a haiku would be a simple meditation on a tree, rather than an agonizing commentary about the evils of root rot. Angst takes a simple grain of rice and transmogrifies it into a tube of toothpaste with the cap lost under a loose tile. Angst is the ultimate excuse. Angst is the opposite of ignorance. Angst is knowing too much. Angst is possessing the right answer when the consensus is wrong. When angst takes the form of a haiku, the expression is a poetic interpretation of the fundamental human expression: What the hell?

This collection of poems has taken the original form of haiku and twisted it into a Gordian knot. No longer is haiku limited to satirizing the middle class—today, no subject escapes scrutiny. Modern life necessitates that people live with unpredictability, but there is no rule that dictates how we should deal with it. Angst is a perpetual presence. Befriend it. Express it poetically.

—ALISON HERSCHBERG

I SMELL SOMETHING FOUL

Oh, what a hammer.
I love banging it on walls.
My thumb is throbbing.

ೲ

Merging in traffic.
Get the hell out of my way.
Dent in my fender.

Frozen food section.
I think I'll have some red meat.
A vegan I'm not.

Spare some change buddy?
A bum on my way to work.
The guilt of living.

Looking at your feet. . .
Your sense of fashion is dead.
Call an ambulance.

൦൦

Look at that tractor.
It cuts the wheat like a god.
Think I'll have some rice.

It's raining like hell.
My mascara is running.
Don't believe the hype.

ෙ෨

Late drinking last night.
I look into the mirror.
There are two of me.

Change for the meter.
Uh, can you break a fiver?
Oh yeah, well screw you.

ဘ

Walking down the street,
Something soft under my shoe.
Remains of the dog.

Try to buy a car,
Salesman drools on my wallet.
Not a chance in hell.

෨

A curious dog.
Wet nose and a silk pants suit.
Four-legged nuisance.

Sunday night laundry.
Twelve apartments, one machine.
Time to play dirty.

The phone rings three times.
I'm not expecting a call.
I just sit and stare.

Out of the car ma'am.
May I see your license please?
You're under arrest.

ೞ

Driving fifty-five.
There's a bump under my tire.
I smell something foul.

May I have this dance?
My partner won't dance with me.
I've got two left feet.

I open the door.
You've got to be kidding me.
I'm a millionaire.

Down and out and cold.
Newspaper for a blanket.
Sleeping on a bench.

୧୨

Please observe the signs.
Please fasten your seatbelts.
Baby in row F.

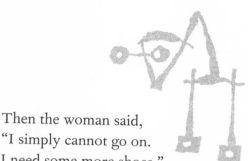

Then the woman said,
"I simply cannot go on.
I need some more shoes."

ꙮꙮ

Look, honey, the mail.
How many bills do you think...
New identity.

A loud grumbling
Coming from under my seat.
Give me a clothespin.

ᏆᏆ

Reruns on TV.
Is there intelligent life?
Oprah, channel five.

Nibble on my neck.
Not now, I've got a headache.
You fill in the blank.

୭୭

Run, run like the wind!
Cops on my tail, gotta go—
Send you a postcard...

Gimme a pint, dude.
White, frothy brew on the bar.
Thank God it's Friday.

The buck will stop here!
As soon as the buck gets here...
Can I have a loan?

The pressure's too high.
I can't take it anymore.
Where's my other sock?

ᕗ

The leaves are turning.
My stomach is turning, too.
A bachelor who cooks.

Taking some time out.
You deserve a break today.
Think I'll give notice.

෨

Golden stream falling.
"What do you think you're doing?"
Bail set at ninety.

A creepy feeling.
Tall dark shadow at my door.
Who let Igor out?

∞

Office politics.
A stranger in a strange land.
Get me outta here.

Driving fifty-five.
Monsoon season upon us.
A sunroof in hell.

જી

Ringing in my ears.
Trouble with the phone system.
I'll just send a note.

I'm going shopping.
I won't use my credit cards.
Well. . . maybe just once.

∞

Checking the want ads.
All the good jobs are taken.
Welcome to Wendy's.

Sparrow overhead.
I told you to wear a hat.
It's a bad hair day.

ෆෆ

Hay fever season.
Pollen and dust in the air.
Ah-choo. Gesundheit.

Swimming in the lake.
Try to do the butterfly.
Help me, I'm drowning.

൭൭

Anniversary.
Box of chocolates and a rose.
Close, but no cigar.

Gas tank is empty.
Try public transportation.
Standing room only.

༖

Shopping for groceries.
A ticket on my windshield.
I just needed eggs.

Tossing and turning.
Got insomnia can't sleep.
I'll try Tequila.

Music in my ears.
Could someone turn off that noise?
I hate Nine Inch Nails.

A change of seasons.
Love and flowers in the air.
Let the games begin.

Sitting at a play.
A hush falls over the crowd.
Somebody breaks wind.

Flowers on my desk.
A secret admirer lurks.
Flowers die slowly.

᭢

On the way to work,
Trucks carrying strange cargo.
Stacked burial vaults.

An office memo:
"Company party bring date."
Standing by the dip.

๑๑

Ant in my kitchen.
Leftovers on the counter.
Exterminator.

Weeding the garden.
A spider under the spade.
Arachnid killer.

∞

Someone else's friends.
Trying to be nice and smile.
I can't stand small talk.

Shopping for some clothes.
Nothing fits me anymore.
I guess it all shrunk.

∽

Dishes in the sink.
Piling high into the sky.
Who's responsible?

Time to pay taxes.
Do your bit for the U.S.
Gimme a tax break.

෴

Hailing a taxi.
No one on the street but me.
Red tail lights recede.

Leaving a message.
I'm stuck in the voice mail loop.
Press five to hang up.

ଚଚ

Friday night dinner.
The family gets together.
Fasten your seatbelt.

Take a vacation.
Don't worry about a thing.
Where's all the luggage?

Asking for a raise.
Rent increase and cost to live.
Who am I kidding?

Can't find my door key.
My luck is running out fast.
Stuck in a cat flap.

☞

Reading a good book.
The suspense is killing me.
The butler did it.

Summer and lycra.
Time for an improved regime.
Save room for dessert.

Running late for work.
Traffic jam on the east bridge.
I should've slept in.

What's inside the fridge?
Haven't opened it for months.
Something is moving.

෯

There's nothing to do.
I've already filed my nails.
Now I'll pick my nose.

The leaves are turning,
And days are getting shorter.
Time to hibernate.

❦

An art opening.
Black and pretense everywhere.
Guess I'll fit right in.

That time of the month.
Leave me alone or I'll kill.
Go on, make my day.

∞

When you're down and out,
And at first you don't succeed—
Stop and have a snack.

Something in my teeth.
Maybe no one will notice.
Poppyseed bagel.

Deadline approaching.
I've got to get this finished.
Think I'll clean the house.

I'm thirsty for tea.
Faulty wiring interferes.
Small kitchen fire burns.

∞

What color lipstick?
There's so many to choose from.
I need some chocolate.

"Could you keep it down?"
Trying to sleep in the 'burbs.
Heavy metal hell.

∽

Got to work early,
Everyone else running late.
Let the sunshine in.

Woke up this morning,
Can't find any of my things.
Nothing here is mine...

Went out to dinner.
Boyfriend paid for everything.
What a go-getter.

Singing Cole Porter,
A man in a blond wig wails.
Another barfly.

∞

The party's over.
Time for everyone to leave.
Someone's in my bed.

Talking on the phone.
Annoying persistent clicks.
I hate call waiting.

ରଚ

Notice in the mail.
"Your balance is negative."
Must be a mistake.

Recycling garbage.
Fate of the world in my hands.
I'm toeing the line.

இ

Voices in my head.
An angel and a devil.
Who's the referee?

57

Someone else's junk.
Bargain prices all around.
Sunday garage sale.

စာ

Getting a hair cut.
Stylist writes gossip column.
I am a blank wall.

I ran out of gas.
God, I caused a traffic jam.
My face is burning.

Father's Day dinner.
Fancy restaurant in town.
Vodka and tonic.

Parade in Fremont.
Naked men on bicycles.
I love Seattle.

෨

Thundercloud above,
Open sandals down below.
In bed with the flu.

Hard crunchy pretzels.
What did you say? I can't hear—
My teeth are breaking.

Flirting on the phone.
Overheard conversation.
Blackmail in the cards.

A co-worker sighs.
Relationship is ending.
Rebounding alert.

೧

Is it hot in here?
My brow is dripping with sweat.
Stop looking at me.

My hands are shaking.
Performance anxiety.
Poetry reading.

❧

Painful cuticles.
Pressure is high, patience low.
Anti-depressant.

Halloween party.
Green lamé bell-bottom flares.
Monday night fever.

꩜

I'm in a hurry,
Got to get it overnight,
Federal Express.

A fig leaf in place.
OK, you can turn around.
Explore your dark side.

༄

Brainstorming session.
Hurricane of ideas.
Get an umbrella.

The sun is shining.
Sunglasses not dark enough.
Retina damage.

My painting's for sale.
A million dollar price tag.
I just can't let go.

What is the question?
I'm not listening to you.
You really bore me.

೦೦

Trendy Birkenstocks.
Granola lunch and dinner.
Moving to Berkeley.

My mom's at my pad.
She's using my computer.
Hope it doesn't crash.

๑๒

There's work to be done.
I know all the secret codes.
Indispensable.

Parked under a tree.
What is that sticky substance?
Blood of a maple.

൭൭

Lunchtime at the beach.
Tall lady walks by with son.
The nannies are out.

A trip to Starbucks.
I'm addicted to the bean.
Somebody help me.

∞

Staring at the screen.
Vision beginning to blur.
Time to take a jog.

Cutting through water.
Rippling, peaceful reflections.
Kayak on the Sound.

Watering my plant.
My green thumb is turning black.
I killed a cactus.

Milkshake from McD's.
I should've had a V-8.
Loosen a button.

∞

The weekend is here.
Rain clouds are rolling in fast.
There goes my picnic.

Dust balls all around.
"No! Wait downstairs, I'll come down!"
For my eyes only.

෨

There's Pez in the bed.
I was sleeping and felt it.
Never eat in bed.

A trip to the zoo.
Lions and tigers and bears.
Oh my, it smells bad.

෨

New shoes on my feet.
I look like the cat's meow.
I feel like a dog.

Breakfast of pancakes,
Bacon the size of redwoods.
Americana.

∞

Driving back and forth.
This is getting redundant.
Tank's empty again.

We are all puppets,
Jerking and swaying like felt.
I have no control.

೦೨

Apartment hunting.
All the good ones are taken.
A room with a view.

Creative thinking.
Felt tip pen and some paper.
Primary colors.

ൟ

Pretentious debate.
The metaphors and clichés…
University.

Social butterfly.
My company in demand.
They all want a piece.

Hot cinnamon roll.
Hanging skin behind my teeth.
Took too big a bite.

Pretty man walks by.
His hair looks better than mine.
Here comes his boyfriend.

൭

Internet access.
Virtual reality.
Bane of existence.

Star Trek on TV.
I want an outfit like that.
I live for reruns.

∽∾

Watching *Melrose Place*.
A dose of reality
Is good for the soul.

The radio blares.
Meaningless words say nothing.
I'm feeling jaded.

∞

I'm trying to sleep.
Boyfriend wants to talk and play.
I am just so tired.

Meaningless filing.
It doesn't matter to me.
They aren't my files.

What's the daily grind?
I'm working for a living.
Java sounds better.

Dreadlocks hanging down.
Beautiful man behind them.
Hello Prince Charming.

᠙᠙

Dinner with some friends.
At least I thought they were friends.
Who needs enemies?

Packing up my stuff.
Rental U-Haul out in back.
Damn, I broke a nail.

෨෧

One small step for man,
One giant leap for mankind.
Thank you, cruise control.

I yawn with fatigue.
Sometimes it's overwhelming.
Hair gel, mousse, or spray?

૭૭

Looked in my closet—
It was a crime of fashion.
Who bought all those clothes?

Defrosted the fridge.
Meat and peas from years ago,
Buried in the ice.

∞

Midnight disaster.
The toilet-seat screws were gone.
I sat down to pee.

Poultry for dinner.
Someone stole all the giblets.
Chicken criminal.

Marijuana smoke.
The smell wafts through the window.
Westfalia van.

A check in the mail.
Sprint wants me to switch over.
I'll do it for cash.

෧෧

I had fish last week—
Time to take the garbage out.
Kitchen smells like trout.

Double tall latte.
Half-decaf, with non-fat milk.
Muffin and a scone.

A knock on my door.
My neighbor's trying to sleep.
Discotheque chez moi.

Business luncheon.
I sat with the client.
He touched me a lot.

๑๑

Having a party.
People sitting on my bed.
Get out of the fridge.

My hands are freezing.
The windows are very thin.
Insulation. Not.

Knee-deep in the muck,
Cows are grazing in the swamp.
Lost my appetite.

Holiday season.
Stores crowded with crazed shoppers.
Gotta have that hat.

ᏏᎧ

Writing poetry
Is no easy task for me.
Where the hell's my muse?

Frisbee in the park.
It was long after sunset.
Caught it with my nose.

๛

Another meeting.
Everyone stammers and coughs.
Autumn leaf floats down.

About the Author

ALISON HERSCHBERG IS AN ARTIST
and writer living in Seattle. She can often be
found wandering in the mountains, painting
the town red, or engaging her contemporaries
in wild-eyed, pointless critique.